30 Da
Your P

C000181775

the step by step guide
to happiness and fulfilment

Chuck Spezzano
Ph.D

ARTHUR JAMES
BERKHAMSTED

This edition published in 1996 by

ARTHUR JAMES LTD
70 Cross Oak Road
Berkhamsted
Hertfordshire HP4 3HZ

A catalogue record for this book is available from the British Library.

ISBN 0 85305 350 2

Typeset in Monotype Bembo by
Pat Saunders, Little Gidding

Printed in Great Britain at the Guernsey Press, Guernsey, C.I.

PREFACE

In this book there is a wealth of tried and accurate information which has worked for thousands of people in my therapeutic practice and seminars over the last two decades. This exploration of your mind can save you pain, time and money, and, of course, assist you in finding your perfect mate.

To put it simply, the process in this book will work if you want it to. There are a number of exercises presented here which have, in and of themselves, manifested partners for people.

The thirty lessons work in two major ways: firstly to make room for a partner in your life, and secondly to invite in your perfect mate. The ideas may be strange and unnatural to your way of thinking at first; don't let that concern you, it's part of the process. You will learn and grow as you go along.

CHUCK SPEZZANO
Hawaii, 1996

DEDICATION

*This book is dedicated with great thanks
to my wife and perfect mate, Lency.*

DAY 1

Your mind is a beautiful thing

Your mind is a beautiful thing because it has limitless potential. Usually our lives are so bound by limits that at times we feel overwhelmed by all we seem to be up against. It is our nature to want to transcend our limits.

Our mind has the ability to heal, to realise truth, to manifest desires, to transcend time, to solve difficult life problems, and much, much more. Most people are afraid of the power of the mind, and remain trapped in situations as if attempting to prove they are powerless. But because I have worked with many thousands of victims, I know the mind's ability to find solutions in the most seemingly impossible situations. When people are really willing to find their way out of a situation, the answer, or at least the doorway to the answer, appears.

The principle of the ego is seek but do not find. This increases your beliefs in scarcity and powerlessness. It has been my study of the mind that has led me to believe and experience that the conscious mind is the mere tip of the iceberg. The rest of the iceberg is made up of the subconscious mind or family patterns and the unconscious mind or ancestral and soul patterns. Besides choice these are the areas that carry self-defeating patterns.

The part of your mind which supplies most of the

answers is the Higher Mind. This is equivalent to the ocean that surrounds the iceberg, our spirit; and this is the best name for the part of our mind which has all the answers. Your whole life will get easier when you begin to work with that part of your mind, because its specific job is to solve your problems and it does so with such speed that it makes it seem as if our conscious mind is part of the problem, rather than, as you might think, part of the solution.

Exercise

Every day write down your answers and thoughts provoked by the exercises. You may like to keep a daily diary of your progress towards your perfect mate.

Choose a problem in your life and write it down as specifically and concretely as your possible can.

Experience any feelings associated with it.

Imagine you are willing and have the courage to find the solution.

DAY 2

The importance of value

Value gives importance. Thus self-value gives you your experience of importance. Your life, your experience, and what the world deals out to you, all reflect your hidden feelings about your own value.

Unfortunately, the bad news is most people value themselves very little. The amount of guilt and unworthiness people experience leads them into sacrifice (which is the kind of giving that blocks receiving), to work hard rather than intelligently, and to live out roles (more of the same kind of giving which allows no receiving, and never lets the giver receive a reward). Roles lead to 'burn-out' and trying to compensate for a lack of self-value. That same lack of self-value drives people into doing, and doing, and doing. It does not allow peace, joy and abundance.

The good news is guilt and unworthiness are not the truth. Guilt is simply a mistake you beat yourself up for. Guilt keeps you stuck. It locks the mistake in place, preventing you from learning the lesson which can be naturally learned from the situation. Guilt causes the lack of self-value you feel; at the deepest psychological levels guilt is a form of avoidance preventing you from growing. But all guilt can be resolved, because ultimately it is a trap set up by the ego.

You deserve a lot more. It is your sense of self-value which ultimately allows you to attract a mate of similar value. Feelings of self-value also create the kind of experience you have with that mate. If you want a perfect mate, you must learn to let yourself be a perfect mate.

Exercise

Today, become aware of what you think of yourself by how you act and by how the world acts towards you.

Notice when you are feeling unhappy and when you are compensating for feeling unhappy by sacrifice, by keeping busy or by seeking mindless pleasure. These activities just hide places of valuelessness.

When you catch yourself in a situation which makes you aware of your lack of self-value, make a new decision about yourself. Each choice you make for your innocence and self-worth will add to your life and natural attractiveness.

DAY 3

The purpose of life

The purpose of life is happiness. Simple enough, but most of us take wrong turns on the Highway to Happiness. When we are not happy, then healing becomes our primary purpose. The purpose of a relationship is firstly happiness, and secondly, to heal. It does this through love, communication and forgiveness. When you are living your purpose you experience fulfilment. Each of us has a personal purpose which only we can fulfil.

Relationships provide the motivation and the fuel for completing our personal purpose – the means for us to reach happiness. They give us the support to heal ourselves as we progress through life. They expose our wounds from the past in order to make our continued growth possible. The past is relived in present relationship patterns, giving us the opportunity for healing. Heartbreak in a relationship has its roots in the past, and is a reliving of a past heartbreak, therefore as the past heartbreak is healed the present one heals too.

Exercise

Let go of your plan for happiness and let your Higher Mind be in charge. If you examine your ego's record of success and happiness in life, you will naturally find yourself motivated to try what your Higher Mind might suggest. Be willing to do anything you are inspired to do, but let your conscious mind be at rest. As you develop a relationship with your Higher Mind, you will become naturally more interdependent with those around you, including the person who will become your perfect mate. This interdependence is a natural prerequisite, not only to finding the perfect mate, but in keeping him or her. Remember your desire for the right relationship is a natural part of your purpose in life. You deserve your perfect mate and you deserve partnership.

DAY 4

You have what you want

With this lesson we begin our first major foray into the subconscious mind. What you have in your life is exactly what you want because that is what you have made and brought to you. The way to have something different is by changing your mind because that allows you to change your world.

One of the biggest traps we face in life is playing the role of victim, thinking we don't want what we have. Once you begin to realise you are making the choices in an instant and then in the next instant repressing them, you can start choosing consciously, and have a much better chance of getting what you really want.

As you begin to explore experiences in your life, especially why you don't have your perfect mate, many feelings may come up: anger, defensiveness, denial, guilt, hurt, doubt, shame, disbelief and sadness. Just experience them and notice you are experiencing them. No negative feeling is ultimately accurate. This principle is the basis of all healing and is the reason why all painful feelings and situations can be transformed.

Exercise

This next exercise helps to discover one's hidden agenda:

Step 1: Pretend for a moment you really don't want a partner! Now, we know you do, but for the purpose of this exercise pretend you don't.

Step 2: Write down all the reasons which come into your mind why you don't want a partner.

Step 3: Consider how what you have written is your subconscious agenda which is stopping you.

Step 4: Choose once again what it is you really want in the light of this new information.

To discover other crucial subconscious motivations that are more important to you than having your perfect mate ask yourself these next questions beginning each one with 'If I were to know …' This allows you to access your intuition to what you have hidden: If I were to know what not having a perfect mate allows me to do, it is … If I were to know what I don't have to do by not having a perfect mate, it is … If I were to know what I'm afraid of or think I would lose by having a perfect mate, it is … If I were to know who I'm getting revenge on or who I think I would be unfaithful to by having a perfect mate, it is … If I were to know what guilt I'm paying off or why I don't deserve a perfect mate, it is because …

When answers arise to these questions it is important to change your mind so you can be open for a perfect mate. If you are willing to change, give these to your Higher Mind for healing.

DAY 5

Saying yes to life

To get what you want, your perfect mate, you will have to change. If you stay as you are, you will go on receiving what you have now. Change is one of the greatest blessings on earth, yet it is fear of change, or fear of the unknown, which most commonly blocks us. But to grow and reach our higher goals we must change.

I've worked with many people who would rather keep the devil they know, even if it is loneliness, than reach for the angel they don't. Years of studying the dynamics of relationship problems have taught me that fear, fear of the next step to be precise, is at the core of all problems.

Since most of your problems have the purpose of delaying your next step in order to protect you from your fear, when you take the next step it resolves the problem you are facing now.

So it takes our trust to step forward, not knowing what the next step is, but reminding ourselves it will be better, just like every other step forward we have ever taken. Of course, taking the 'next step' isn't literally taking a step. It is being open to change, saying 'yes' to life. When this happens, life actually will change around us. One powerful way to look at life is to regard our major problems as fear of taking the next developmental step in life. That will help us to focus on the real issue rather than its numerous and confusing symptoms.

Exercise

Sit quietly and close your eyes.

Imagine the next step awaits you and you can say 'yes' to it, 'yes' to change. You don't have to figure out what it is, or how to do it. All you have to do is want it, be willing for it to happen, knowing it will be better and further forward than where you are now. Take one step at a time.

Say YES to the next step. Say YES to your perfect mate.

DAY 6

Opening the door

Once, years ago, I broke up with a girlfriend. Our relationship had begun as a friendship and became something more. I had always thought we would retain that friendship no matter what happened. But when we did breakup I felt that everything was lost. I can remember how angry I was at first, but I soon got over it.

I began looking around for eligible dating partners. It seemed as if all the eligible women had moved out of the city. I was a young doctor, athletic, romantic, attractive enough. Yet there were no eligible women around. I couldn't understand it.

Four and a half months went by, which was a record for me in not finding and dating someone I found attractive. At that time I became a support staff member at a three-and-a-half day workshop. On the very last day of the workshop, while thinking of my lack of dating partners, I had an intuitive flash that I had slammed the relationship door at the end of the last one. I realised that was the reason I had met no one. So I decided to open the door and within the hour I had met someone I was attracted to, who let me know that she was very available. Within a week, I met two more very eligible dating partners and proceeded to make up for lost time.

This taught me a very important principle: relationships wait on invitation and not on time; your perfect mate awaits your invitation, not just a special time or place.

Exercise

If you are not in a serious relationship, or haven't been in one for a while, take a look to see if you have slammed the door of relationships on your perfect mate – maybe after your last relationship, or even as a child with your parents.

Imagine that you can feel or see the door inside you which you closed. See yourself walking to that door and doing whatever it takes to open it. Remember this is your door: it will be any way you picture it. And as you open it you will experience a new openness which can last.

Ask yourself: 'Am I ready for my perfect mate, or do I want more time to learn and build up confidence with light relationships along the way?'

It is important to accept wherever you are, as this will, paradoxically, help you to unfold and advance.

DAY 7

The power of forgiveness

Many people prevent their perfect mate finding them because they are holding on to major grievances against their parents or old lovers. Such grievances lock you in the past. The anger or withdrawal that occurred then stops you from realising your present possibilities. Forgiveness frees us from the past.

Sometimes sacrifice is confused with forgiveness. People become afraid to forgive because they think if they do forgive, what they don't like will continue to happen to them. That is sacrifice, not forgiveness. Forgiveness releases you from the situation you don't want so that both the forgiver and the forgiven are freed. Forgiveness is the solvent that releases the super-glue of grievances and guilt.

Judgement and grievance always hide subconscious guilt. All forgiveness then, in truth, is self-forgiveness. Forgiveness releases the guilt, conscious or sub-conscious, which is part of every problem that holds us back. Grievances and guilt are distracting and can stop personal growth. Transform them through forgiveness and thus free yourself from unpleasant behaviour patterns which block your ability both to attract and to receive.

Exercise

Today, allow to come to mind any problems or grievances, from the past or present, which may be holding you back from your perfect partnership. Under every problem or grievance is hidden guilt.

Allow the person, or persons, you need to forgive to come into your mind. Ask yourself: 'Would I blame myself for this?' If not you both are released.

Be willing to free yourself and the person you are forgiving from the destructive power of that hidden guilt. Forgiveness releases us from that which we blame on others and ourselves.

Because we always want to be right (which hides guilt and destroys happiness) we are poor at forgiving others. But the easiest form of forgiveness is when you become willing for it to be accomplished and turn it over to your Higher Mind.

DAY 8

Feeling your feelings!

Your feelings add richness and dimension to your life and make you more attractive. You don't have to feel your feelings to manifest your perfect mate, but you do if you want to enjoy a long and happy relationship. Your ability to feel your feelings correlates with your ability to enjoy yourself, to be a good partner and to commit yourself to a relationship. But I want you to make a distinction between feeling your feelings and the amount of feeling you display.

Some people avoid their true feelings by expressing many kinds of other feelings. This can become a form of hysteria. Negative emotions are sometimes used as blackmail or revenge, or as a form of tantrum or immaturity, depending on the way they are expressed. But just as an over-emphasis on your feelings or the expression of negative feeling can be counter-productive to good relationships and a form of avoidance, so can dissociation from your feelings.

A successful relationship is possible when we move from dependence and independence with others into interdependence. As we get in touch with our feelings we become more able to relate. Part of the movement from independence towards interdependence is being able to re-associate ourselves with our feelings and our body. And as we get in touch with our negative feelings and release them, our ability to receive and experience increases.

Exercise

One of the simplest forms of healing is to experience your negative feelings or emotions until they disappear. You can do this whenever you are not feeling great.

All you do is allow yourself to feel the feelings as intensely as possible, even exaggerate them.

Observe everything about your feelings, explore the minute and distinct sensation of each emotion. You will find that as you do they will begin to shift.

Once started, don't stop until you are feeling great. Feelings, even the most chronic ones, have an end.

Practice feeling your feelings all day today. You can do that and do everything else.

Today, and at least once every day, pick a time when you are not feeling good. Feel and follow all the layers of feeling through until you are feeling really good.

DAY 9

The truth will set you free!

Many people are frightened of relationships because they are afraid of sacrifice. They fear they will become a 'love-slave' the way they did in the past, and that is enough to keep anybody independent. Independence eventually leads to dissociation and deadness.

Yet the extent of your independence is a reflection of the amount of sacrifice and dependency you still need to heal.

Roles begin in childhood with a trauma or some kind of emotional loss which was never resolved or mourned. The role becomes a pattern which typically repeats itself in your life. All three roles – sacrifice, dependency and independence – are surreptitious forms of taking combined with an inability to receive. This may involve giving in order to take or losing now to win later or withdrawing so as not to be taken from. If we fail to resolve these counter-productive roles, deadness in our relationships is the inevitable result.

Not knowing how to handle deadness and boredom keeps many people out of committed relationships, or relationships altogether. Yet for a successful relationship and life you have to learn these lessons.

One of the easiest ways to move through feelings of

deadness is just to be more willing to move forward in your life. Fear of the next step leads to a sameness that is deadening. It is the willingness to move forward which creates change, because life changes as you become ready for it to change.

Another simple but lifesaving way to move through roles and deadness or any problem is to ask who needs your help. Imagine the problem as a wall between you and them that can be moved through as you *choose* to move through it and join them. This joining puts both of you in a successful flow.

Exercise

Today, use truth as an indicator of your happiness. Truth is a major antidote to feelings of deadness. When something feels dead, truth is being avoided. Happiness is our deepest, truest consciousness; if you are feeling unhappy, it is not the truth. As our problems are resolved, we are led to happiness and as our consciousness grows, so does our happiness. If you are not happy, ask for the truth to be shown to you.

Seek the truth. Desire the truth. It will set you free.

Today the truth will be shown to you by something outside you or inside you if you really want it. Choose the truth and you will find your freedom.

DAY 10

Letting go of the past opens up the present

Once again we have reached a seminal lesson in the process of finding your perfect mate – the principle of letting go. Letting go counters the destructive influence of holding on.

Holding on, or attachment, is need in the disguise of love. It is a form of counterfeit love which leads to a blurring of personal boundaries between you and the one to whom you are attached. This leads to fusion and sacrifice, which create feelings of deadness in relationships. The extent of your attachment in relationships is the extent of your unattractiveness, and repels your partner. What keeps you attractive in a relationship is your letting go of attachment and needs.

But you must distinguish letting go from throwing away, or dissociation. Letting go is a willingness to give up our attachments, so you can feel connection and love with your partner. When your partner becomes independent and needs more space, you are becoming dependent and are called upon to let go. Whenever you let go, your relationship can move forward to the next step in partnership, confidence and love.

Exercise

Imagine you could measure what percentage you are holding on to of past relationships by negative or positive emotions. It must include family members also. If you are needy or independent it is a sure sign of holding on. To have a new relationship in the present the old relationships must be let go of for you to be available.

Today is a great day for letting go of old relationships; here are some ways to do it:

Experience any negative feelings until only a positive feeling is left from the past.

Forgive.

Take the next step.

Recognise living in the past is destructive, and choose to live in the present.

Give up attachment, so you can have love.

Turn these relationships over to your Higher Mind to let go for you.

DAY 11

You can have what you want
– if you want what you have!

Today we will look at two very important concepts: acceptance and letting go.

The title has a double significance about acceptance. If you accept what you have, therefore, you naturally have what you want, but also if you do not resist what you have then what you want can come to you. What you resist persists. When you resist what you have, everything jams and cannot move forward.

Conversely, what you accept changes. Acceptance is not a form of apathy, but an active principle for healing resistance and pain.

Acceptance gets our lives moving again when they have become stuck; the power of acceptance moves life forward. Sometimes because of hurt, heartbreak or feelings of rejection, we keep ourselves defended or quit relationships altogether.

Hurt does not come from what others do or don't do to us but from how we react to what they do. When we finally realise the truth – whether or not someone else is rejecting us – it is *our* rejection of ourselves, others or the situation itself which creates the hurt, then we are in charge of our feelings.

Exercise

Review your life for major hurts.

Choose to accept, rather than deny or hide them, so that where your life has stopped it can begin to unfold again.

Affirm that being stopped by these old hurts is not what you want.

Become aware of any urgency or feelings of 'have to' or 'need to' have a partner. These are expectations and demands which block relationships. It is a sure sign of non-acceptance. Accept where you are but choose to have a perfect partner. Choice and acceptance work together for good.

DAY 12

Guilt, unworthiness and fear are merely illusions

All negative emotions are illusions. Certainly we experience them and they affect us and sometimes even kill us. But, the good news is, these feelings are an illusion.

Painful feelings are an indication that something is amiss. I've worked with tens of thousands of people around the world and I have yet to find anyone, with any kind of willingness, who was unable to resolve the blackest guilt, the deepest pain or the greatest fear.

The basis of the mind is happiness, or wholeness, and it is that wholeness which allows and promotes our continued movement towards growth and healing.

I've encountered many people who thought they were to blame for problem situations in their families while they were growing up, or for other dilemmas they encountered in life. They thought they were so guilty that they did not deserve to have a partner.

I've met many others who thought so poorly about themselves they believed they were unworthy of a partner. Others, who wanted a partner, were afraid to have one, because they felt they were too inadequate to be intimate. They were afraid that when their partners got to know them, they would leave them.

These feelings can be corrected fairly easily. Know that even though you are experiencing such feelings they are not accurate. These feelings, which can block you from finding a partner and destroy relationships, are not the truth. They can be resolved if you are willing to find the way past them, and change, so your life can be better.

Exercise

Make a personal inventory of all the negative feelings which may stop you from finding your perfect mate.

Don't make a monument to a mistake. Don't let mistakes be the superglue which stops you moving forward. If you are willing to change, a better life awaits you. Choose the truth.

Be willing to have a new perception of situations where you are in pain. Pain is an indication of misperception. Your Higher Mind can give you a perception where no one is to blame, not even you.

Ask yourself: 'What has been my purpose in holding on to the old pain?'

Now make a choice as to whether your being right about how you experienced situations and the lack of love and success it entails is more important to you than learning the truth and being successful and happy.

DAY 13

Freeing yourself from your life of fantasy

Here's another important lesson about how you may be blocking yourself from finding your perfect mate.

Everyone this side of enlightenment fantasises. There is nothing wrong with fantasising. In fact most human experience takes place in the imagination. When we think we need something, we fantasise. We begin to daydream about it. When we are hungry, we begin to think about food and notice all the cues related to food around us. Fantasy is an attempt to make up for what is missing within, or outside, you and gives a certain small satisfaction. But it does not really work because it is a defence and all defences cause the very thing you are attempting to defend yourself against.

If you fantasise about your perfect mate, you will often give yourself enough satisfaction; you won't bother to open yourself up for a real relationship. Also, you can create a level of dissatisfaction within a relationship with the continued use of fantasy. Fantasy is using your imagination to make up for something missing.

Fantasy is generated from loss, pain, grievance and the judgement that something is missing in your life. Fantasy is an attempt to provide something that can only be achieved by joining with your partner at a new level of intimacy. Fantasy hides the crucial need to take the next step. When you fantasise, you are stuck and attempting to be satisfied by an illusion. Ultimately it won't work. Let go of your fantasies so you can experience the real thing in a way that satisfies you.

Exercise

Step 1: When you catch yourself in a fantasy today, find out what is underneath it. Somewhere it is hiding a painful feeling which is acting as a wedge between you and your partner.

Step 2: Let go of any painful feeling by experiencing it until it is complete, or by handing it over to your Higher Mind.

Step 3: Recognise the pain for which your fantasies are compensating before turning them, especially those involving your perfect mate, over to your Higher Mind.

DAY 14

If it hurts, it isn't love

Contrary to many popular and traditional songs, love does not hurt, but 'needs' do. Your past heartbreaks were really frustrations of your needs – part of a power struggle, where you used your hurt as a form of emotional blackmail to force your partner to do what you wanted and meet your needs. Your heartbreaks are really acts of revenge through which your pain declares the true, terrible character of your partner.

When you understand the dynamics of hurt and rejection you can take a giant stride towards maturity and you will open up to relationships, and to being a better partner, once you find your mate. Hurt is an attempt to make someone wrong. It results from something you cannot accept, that you resist, or reject. What you push away from you creates the hurt and emotional pain. Then, guess what, you project the pushing away on to your partner and feel rejected.

Projection is a defence. Projection is taking something you are doing and accusing someone else of doing it. Hurt results from giving in order to take, a form of sacrifice used to coerce your partner. When your partner pushes you away for taking, you get upset, which hides what you are doing.

Using hurt or heartbreak as part of your conspiracy to

gain control and thus do what you want in life, can be harmful to you both in finding a relationship and keeping one healthy.

Exercise

If you have any experience which still hurts, discover the control that hurt is giving you. Would you rather have that control, or the perfect mate?

DAY 15

Trust

Trust is one of the cornerstones of a relationship. There is no love without trust. Trust is the opposite of naivety, which is denial parading as innocence. When you trust you turn the power of your mind towards that which you are trusting, in an attitude of confidence, power and success. Trust is one of the core healing principles. Trust can resolve any problem.

A problem comes about because, given the nature of your subconscious, your mind is split. Whenever you are hurt in a major way, you fragment a piece of your mind and reject that part as painful. The fragmented part is projected outward and comes back to meet you as the problem. When this happens you adopt an attitude of control to keep the pain away from you. When you put trust into a negative situation, it begins to work for you and the situation unfolds in a positive way that reintegrates the fragments.

Control is a subtle form of power struggle which blocks relationships and indicates a fear of intimacy. It is the opposite of trust. Control attempts to take into its own power that which trust brings about by opening things up and clearing the way for resolution.

Exercise

Possibly there is a part of you which wants a relationship and another which is afraid to have one.

Imagine holding these two parts, one in each hand.

Feel their weight and texture.

See or sense their colour, size and shapes.

Smell their aromas.

Hear any sounds they make.

Imagine they are melting down to their pure energy – the basic building block of the universe.

Notice that when they are completely melted down the two handfuls are exactly the same.

Join the two handfuls of energy, so that when they are completely joined your fingers are interlocked.

Notice that the new feeling, or form, emerging from the integration gives you your mind back – whole.

Whenever you think of your upcoming partner put your faith and trust in their coming and being your perfect partner. Your trust, which is the power of your mind, must be used towards something, so why not the solution?

DAY 16

Manifesting your life

This is one of the three most important seminal lessons in finding your perfect mate. Do it well!

To manifest something you simply make what you want to happen. We do it all the time subconsciously. People who are good at manifesting what they want are those who know they have the power and use it consciously.

Everything, including negative situations, happens because we choose it. Today's lesson could change the rest of your life if you make this principle a part of your life.

Manifesting is choosing to have something occur and it does. You could be choosing what you want to have happen at any time of day. The times the mind is most receptive are in the twilight sleep zones: just before you fall asleep and just before you get up.

That's the time to tell yourself the kinds of feelings and experiences you want to have during the coming day or in the near future. If you find something occurs which you do not like, then choose your preference again.

Choose situations in which everyone wins, and keep your integrity.

Exercise

See and feel yourself with your perfect mate. You can even see some of the qualities you want but also leave areas to be happily surprised.

Experience the energy of your request, how good it feels, and send it out into the universe, knowing your partner will soon be there. Then let go of your request.

Any time you think of your partner, know your partner is coming to you. Have gratitude both for what you have and what is coming. Don't worry about not doing it exactly right. It is not the way that you do it which counts, but your intention. I've heard of at least half a dozen ways of doing this and they all worked. This is the essence. When you have finished let your Higher Mind handle it for you. You may develop a style which works better for you. Trust yourself. And good luck.

DAY 17

Your attitude is your direction

Your attitude is the most fundamental aspect of your life because it defines your direction. Your attitude is made up of your decisions, all moving in the same general direction. It's important to know what you want, where you want to go, to set goals, and make good decisions to support those goals (and you may have to be courageous and take a few risks).

You will need to change for you to have your perfect mate, or even for you to be happy with your perfect mate. Change is inevitable if you want to succeed, because – just think for a moment – if you go on doing what you've been doing, you'll go on getting more of what you've already got. Your attitude towards change is crucial to your success. If you are in pain, or feeling the deadness, you may begin to recognise change as the greatest blessing on earth. Why don't you just decide that change will be an exciting adventure?

It is important to choose not only to have your perfect mate, but to be happy with him or her. This may seem obvious, but without choosing that second goal your first major misunderstanding may be your last. Once you have chosen your goal for the relationship anything which comes up is just something to work out on your way to happiness.

There are problems and situations to work on and heal in every relationship. Everything between you and total joy will come up between you and your partner, because old pain and behaviour patterns disguise themselves as problems in present relationships and lead us into fights or deadness. Have the healing attitude in your relationship, that if anything is not love it calls for help.

Make sure you and your partner always win 100 per cent. If you don't, you will end up paying the bill, by sacrifice or by the loss of your partner's attractiveness. Choose to learn joyfully and remove that which separates you and your partner.

Exercise

Take a long look at your life. What do you need to change or learn? It's time to change, to eliminate choices, prejudices or fears which may be holding you back. Choose goals and attitudes for your relationship that will most support your mutual growth and happiness.

Probably the most important thing you can do before and after you have your mate is to turn the relationship over to your Higher Mind for direction. This ensures that you are always heading in a direction of healing and happiness rather than using your needs to punish and attack your partner.

DAY 18

Free your family, free yourself

All of us have major family patterns which determine our relationship patterns. Without healing our family patterns we are either doomed to repeat the same family patterns, overcompensate for them in deadening roles or stay out of relationships altogether. Even with a certain amount of awareness, unless we have dedicated our relationship to our Higher Mind for use in healing and wholeness, we will then dedicate it to attempting to serve our needs which will destroy our relationship. Unless we are dedicated to healing, we will hold our partner hostage to our past pain, giving them the job of making up for it for us. This will destroy our relationships and make them a hell instead of the quickest way to heaven.

We all have a soul purpose that our life is meant for. We have come to heal and transcend certain problems. In so doing we find that we have a natural gift that extends to others because of who we are. The pattern for fulfilling this purpose and our greatness is already existent in our families. It is what we came to heal. It is the problems that we came to save our parents and family from. Yet the family is a morass of guilt, blame, sacrifice and heartbreak that both obscures our purpose and perpetuates the problems generations afterwards.

The very problems that we have come to heal we accuse ourselves of. But this is hidden under layers of heartbreak, blame or sacrifice. If we do not return ourselves and our families to balance, and give each of our family members the gift we came to give them, we are doomed to carry their wounds through our life. This is no less ruinous if the wounds are dramatically evident or hidden away under sacrifice and other forms of compensation. This is what sets up the core patterns of our subconscious mind, effecting both relationship and success.

Exercise

This next exercise can be used to heal past and present trauma and heartbreak. Every painful situation now will have a root in the past. Imagine your parents or others in the past at the times that were most painful to you in your life. Ask your Higher Mind to carry you all back to your centre, a place of balance that is full of peace, innocence and grace. This heals the guilt, sacrifice and fusion patterns and removes the pain of unmet needs. Next imagine that a door in your heart and mind was opening so that the very gift necessary to heal and transcend the situation extends to whoever is there. This ends the separation and thus the pain at this level, and it anchors the gift that you have come to give those around you and the world at large, bringing you joy and fulfilment.

DAY 19

Roles, rules and duties

Roles and duties are about doing the right things for the wrong reasons. We drop into roles for approval, perform our expected duties to prove we are good, and to show others, usually our parents, how they should have acted in order to treat us right.

Roles and duties are based on grievances, feelings of guilt and failure. They are embodied forms of sacrifice and compensate us for our painful feelings.

Roles are like suits of armour, encasing us, cutting us off from intimacy, our ability to give and receive. Roles create deadness. The two most common roles are 'being good' and 'being a hard worker'.

Giving and receiving increases our sense of self-worth and heals the main dynamic of fear of commitment, which is that no one, including ourselves, is worthy of continuous attention.

Rules are built on guilt and pain. They have the same dynamics as roles and duties. They are rigid demands on ourselves and others, which lead to no-win situations, because if someone follows your rules, you feel a bit safer but still have the fear that generated those rules. Rules are counterfeit principles.

Exercise

*Look for all the areas in which you are giving, but don't seem
to be receiving. Giving and receiving are a natural cycle, giving
leads to receiving. An area where you are not receiving is an
area in which you are in a role. To change a role into true
giving just choose to give rather than giving because you are
supposed to.*

*Make a list of all your rules which apply to the areas where you
would feel hurt, upset or insulted if your rules weren't kept,
e.g. infidelity, tardiness, insensitivity. To find these rules,
think back to the times you felt hurt. As you find your rules,
make new choices about the ones you feel ready to let go of.*

*A rule hides old pain and guilt and is really a defence begging
to be attacked so that the pain and guilt can be healed.
Typically, when a rule is broken and we experience pain in a
relationship, we adopt a reactive, defensive or attacking posture
to protect ourselves rather than using the opportunity for
communication, healing and evolution.*

DAY 20

Family roles

Family roles can stop you having your perfect mate. They can block many of the good things in life. The major family roles are the hero, the martyr, the scapegoat, the lost child and the charmer. The hero, martyr and scapegoat are all guilt induced, while the lost child and charmer are generated by feelings of inadequacy. While the hero and charmer are successful roles they don't allow receiving.

The hero is the shining light in the family, always succeeding, always winning, being good at sports, getting excellent grades, etc. The scapegoat takes on and becomes the problem person in the family. The martyr becomes sick or has problems in an attempt to swallow everyone's pain and save the family. Charmers, or mascots, entertain the family with their humour and play. The lost or invisible child tries to disappear to help the family.

All these roles are forms of giving without receiving. A family apportions different jobs to its members in an unsuccessful attempt to find balance and save itself. The more a family is caught up in roles, the more dysfunctional it is; and the more dysfunctional a family is, the more it will get caught in roles. It is a vicious circle.

The martyr, scapegoat and lost child roles may be especially destructive to beginning a relationship. Martyrs and scapegoats may not have time enough to focus on a relationship if they are still caught in family roles. And a lost child may not have enough self-esteem to even try.

Exercise

Take a look at your family. Which roles did everyone play?

Be willing to make new choices if these roles are not serving you. As you find a new balance, your family will too.

Do not use your family or anyone else to hold you back from your own life and a relationship. These roles are defences that won't succeed. Give up your roles and keep asking the truth to be shown to you.

DAY 21

Nothing is hard if you give it

This is another way of saying commitment, giving yourself, opens you up to receive everything you want. I have dealt with this concept a good number of times in hundreds of seminars and workshops. Usually it is fear, guilt, unworthiness, holding on or sacrifice which prevent people having what they want. There is always some kind of ambivalence present: if you were not half-hearted you would have your true partner.

From observing the dynamics of thousands of people, one of the core reasons we don't allow ourselves to have it all – love, money, sex, success, etc. – is because we would be embarrassed to win so much and be so lucky and successful. We are afraid of having to deal with envy and attack, and so too often we give up on our gifts and talents. We literally make ourselves smaller to fit in with the rest of the crowd.

But having given up our natural gifts, and thus surrendered our leadership qualities and uniqueness, we still want to be special in everyone else's eyes. We become competitive, trying to keep our partners small so we are not threatened by their greatness, and then attacking them if they don't treat us as special, which is a form of counterfeit love that is very destructive. What we are not giving we demand from our partner. There can only be a problem if there is something we are not giving.

Exercise

Today, let's re-examine ambivalence. Answer the following questions and as answers or thoughts come to you intuitively write them down.

What specifically holds you back from having your true partner?

What style do you have that chases partners away?

What is it you are afraid of?

What do you think you would lose if you got a partner?

What do you feel too guilty about to have your true partner?

Why don't you deserve your true partner?

Who would be too jealous of you if you got your perfect partner?

Any answer which came up is not the truth! It is a belief you have used against yourself to stop you. You can choose to change it with the help of your Higher Mind.

Imagine that you have found the part of you that you have refused to give. Become that part and tell yourself why you don't want to give yourself. At the end of this exercise you might choose to give yourself where you have withheld yourself.

DAY 22

Healing power struggles

Power struggles are the major stumbling block to an unfolding relationship. If a couple does not learn how to transcend their power struggles, they are unlikely to succeed in their relationship. Many people are afraid of venturing into a committed relationship because they do not think they will survive the fighting, or deadness, caused by competition, which is a subtle form of power struggle.

In power struggles, we typically make the biggest mistake in a relationship. We think the other person has been put on earth solely for the purpose of taking care of our needs. We cover this up during the romance stage, but it emerges in force in the power struggle stage, when we fight to have things done our way, which we believe is the 'right way'. We give our partners ultimatums to do it 'my way or take to the highway'. We fight for control. We fight to be the most independent one. We fight to have our needs met first, or twice if our partner is not too tired. A power struggle is a fight to get our partners to meet our needs.

If we do not change our attitude about our needs as a place for healing rather than a place for controlling or attacking our partner we are dooming ourselves to the delay of moving forward to healing and happiness or the destruction of the relationship. Even when we succeed in controlling our partner to meet our needs they become less attractive to us. To succeed there must be a goal of both of you winning 100 per cent and using needs as a place for healing rather than fighting. Every fight which is only ever to have our own needs met is always a fear of the success and lack of control of the next step.

Exercise

Think carefully about anyone you are fighting with, or fought with in the past.

What step forward were you afraid of?

What was the gift, or the new level, you turned away from out of fear?

That step, that gift, that new level is still waiting for you. Be willing to receive this gift or new level for yourself and for all those you love. The step you take now is a gift to your future partner that helps them step forward, that helps them step towards you.

DAY 23

Transforming boredom

Boredom stops relationships! People are afraid of commitment to a relationship for fear of dying a slow and painful death from boredom. Boredom is easily resolved by taking an emotional risk in communication or intimacy with your partner! Such risks create new levels of emotional and sexual excitement.

But when we withhold ourselves, usually from fear because we are trying to keep ourselves safe, we end up bored.

The biggest source of boredom in a relationship comes from sacrifice masquerading as love. Everybody has confused sacrifice with love. Sacrifice is counterfeit love. The sacrificer gives, but does not receive. Love is naturally giving and receiving. Giving without receiving leads to 'burn-out' and deadness. Receiving leads to giving at a whole new level.

Sacrifice does not work and bogs down a relationship. It is a form of compromise or adjustment to a situation that needs healing, or resolving, through open and honest communication, otherwise both partners will feel they have lost.

Sacrifice is actually a way of avoiding intimacy and mutuality. It is a surreptitious form of taking in the future by sacrifice now. It is a way of taking care of others' needs now so your needs can be taken care of in the future. It disregards healing and joining in love and thus it adjusts and continues the needy and unsuccessful situation.

Exercise

All sacrifice is based on past and present grievances, against someone you felt did not do it right for you. Your sacrifice is an attempt to show how it should have been done.

List all the sacrifice situations you can remember from when you were a child right up to today so you can discover the hidden grievances.

Forgive those people so you don't imprison yourself in sacrifice.

Next, today or any day you find yourself in boredom, take a risk. Communicate, find where you have been withholding yourself and share yourself.

DAY 24

Commitment – the gateway to freedom

I would like to introduce a notion which single, independent people don't even begin to suspect and which people in committed relationships know: commitment brings freedom generating truth and ease.

Independent people are afraid commitment is a kind of slavery. The spectre of sacrifice is one of the major reasons, ranking alongside old heartbreak and jealousy, why people stay single, carefully guarding their independence. Unfortunately, being independent solves nothing – it only hides problems. Independence is the extent that we are afraid of intimacy and inter-dependence.

Commitment brings freedom into existence leading a couple into the truth and ease of real partnership. Miraculously, because a relationship is a team effort and the success of one is enjoyed by both, it only takes one partner to choose commitment to move the couple on to the next step in partnership.

Commitment is prioritising. Because commitment makes your partner more important than your needs and your conflicts, it resolves them. Together with trust, forgiveness and a number of other major healing choices, commitment has the power to shift any problem completely.

Exercise

Today, adopt a new attitude towards commitment because it is what you give in any situation that determines your experience of it. When you give the best of yourself in a relationship you will feel you are the one who is having the best.

Choose a situation, or person, with whom you seem to be in conflict, or where you feel deadness.

Decide to give 100 per cent to that person or situation and witness the change. You'll know how much you have given by how the relationship enlivens. Our partners never fail unless we stop giving to them.

DAY 25

As you believe, so shall it be

Nothing can happen to you unless you believe it can. Our beliefs make up a matrix which we project out on to the world, which returns looking as if it is what is really happening in the world. If you change your mind, you can literally change the world.

Discovering and examining our beliefs is one of the easiest ways to get into our subconscious to change it. In any situation ask yourself intuitively: 'What do I believe that could make this happen?' Your intuitive mind is a far better tool for this purpose than your analytical mind because it allows information to pop into your mind. For instance, if your partner has treated badly, ask yourself: 'What must I believe about my partner, relationships and the opposite sex that this could happen?'

Your feelings originate from your beliefs, thoughts and values. If you believe the opposite sex will reject you, then you are probably overly self-conscious around them because you are afraid of being rejected yet again!

But, here's the bad news, the nature of fear is that whatever you fear you are already feeling. So if you are afraid of rejection, you are feeling rejected. When you feel rejected, you act rejected and that leads to rejectable behaviour.

Be comforted; anyone with any willingness at all can move successfully through deeply held beliefs like this into fulfilling and happy relationships.

Today, consider your relationship situation.

List the beliefs you must have had for the situation to be the way it is.

If you don't like the situation or the beliefs, make a choice which will serve you better. Beliefs can easily be changed. As soon as you realise you have them, make another choice about what you want.

DAY 26

Do you want your relationship or your story?

Your personality has been putting together your life story for years. Typically, it is filled with painful and heroic episodes all neatly tied together to prove what a good person you are.

Anything you try hard to prove means you believe the opposite. If I were to attempt to convince you how bright I am, pretty soon you would begin to suspect that either I was insecure about my intelligence or that I was unintelligent. Our stories or concepts about ourselves are the most primordial aspects of ourselves that limit joy and generate all our victim patterns and problems with our families and other relationships.

Our life stories are largely composites of victim and martyr stories. Suffering is a veiled form of attack and so this is a way of feigning innocence while attacking. This is not an easy area to explore because typically we keep it all hidden from our conscious mind. Our story is all-consuming. We are the heroes and heroines, but the problem is that the natural reward for all our good, or heroic actions, does not go to us: it goes to our story. It is the movie of our life. Another problem with our stories in general is that as the hero or heroine we tend to make those around us the *supporting* actors and actresses in our story. They are naturally doing the same with us and this leads to problems.

In general, we are all called to change the victim, tragic, horror and heartbreak stories into healing, happy and love stories.

Exercise

Begin to examine your story, the one you are writing in your life, especially where it covers relationships.

Take ten minutes to write at least a page about your relationship story or tell it to a friend or dictate it to a tape recorder. Begin with asking yourself: 'If my relationship story were a movie, what would the title be?'

Pick out the key patterns which repeat again and again or which run through your story.

What are you trying to prove by your story?

If you don't like what you've found, make some new decisions about what you want.

DAY 27

Grace of intimacy

One of our great fears in life is the fear of intimacy. Intimacy is joining with someone – moving through all your blocks, considerations and fears to a heartfelt closeness.

Intimacy, which is love made manifest, has the power and grace to heal all problems because one of the core aspects to unlocking any problem is that there is always separation present. For instance, when we fall ill there is a part of us which feels cut off and unloved. If we can find and integrate that part, the illness disappears. The power of intimacy and love allows a grace which transforms problems easily to become manifest.

Intimacy seems to be everything we ever wanted, but we are afraid of our own sense of inadequacy and unworthiness, or we are afraid we will lose ourselves if we join with another.

Intimacy is not romance, which is based on our dreams about the other; it is a real sharing of heart, mind and energy in such a way that we move forward confidently. When we are prepared to take the next step in intimacy it has the same effect as saying 'yes' to life. We move forward; we grow.

One technique which makes intimacy more possible is

simply being with, or moving towards your partner without judgement, until you feel mutuality and 'joining'. When you join your partner with love, problems and their symptoms seem to disappear and a new grace and confidence appear. Your level of intimacy is your level of both availability and attractiveness. When you have achieved intimacy you are utterly winsome to those around you.

Exercise

Today, find someone to 'join' with in order to help that person, to help yourself, or to help you both. Don't stop until you feel the release that intimacy brings.

Keep moving towards them until you join them and feel joy and peace.

Practise this as often as you can, for it will empower you to move forward in your relationship whatever the nature of the problem.

DAY 28

Feel the joy

Most people think that first you find a partner and then you feel joyful. Actually, it works the other way round. Your partner comes along because a level of energy and joy, which is hugely attractive, begins to well up inside you and attracts your perfect mate.

The more you feel joy the more beautiful you become. Just like when spring arrives and all the flowers begin to bloom, so naturally the bees appear.

So much would just come to us if we chose joy first and let that be a part of our lives. If you are joyful, you have already achieved the purpose of a relationship.

Joy is a choice we can make all the time instead of choosing our stories. It is a choice for love instead of fear. At a subconscious level, every problem we have has the purpose of causing something to happen that will bring us joy.

Your partner can never succeed in *making* you happy because of the nature of expectations and demands. Make no demands, have no expectations. Instead, give all you can and love all you can, especially in those areas where you want things from your partner, because that will create joy and receiving in your relationship. Your joy is the best gift you can give your partner. It is magnetic and enchanting.

Exercise

Today, if you experience anything other than joy, say to yourself: 'I could be feeling joy instead of this.'

At the beginning of the day, and at every hour, choose joy.

DAY 29

Temptations – accept no substitutes

For a number of years I have noticed women coming to my seminars hoping to find a partner. Often they blossomed in joy, but the next time I visited their country they were dejected and depleted once more. Some time ago I decided to take a closer look at what was going on.

I found out that they had found the perfect mate within a fortnight, except for one thing – he was married or in another relationship. Was it coincidence, or bad karma, or was something else afoot? Within six months I had the answer.

When you are wide open in joy, the personality doesn't have much to stop you with, so it offers you a last trap. Along comes a *simulated* Mr or Ms 100 per cent perfect. They are really Mr or Ms 85 per cent perfect because they are in another relationship. But, if you have not had someone to love and be loved by for a long time, the temptation is seemingly irresistible and you fall into the trap of a triangular relationship. This is a horrible trap which causes guilt and delays happiness.

The usual scenario is that when you are wonderfully wide open you choose Mr or Ms 85 per cent and completely miss The Real Mr or Ms 100 per cent because you have now become deeply involved in the triangular relationship. Sometimes you notice the 100 per cent possibilities but miss their importance because you are already lured into the trap.

Now, when I see women leaving my workshop in that starry-eyed way, I give them my best advice: if they meet Mr 85 per cent, I say enjoy the connection and friendship, but don't get involved romantically because Mr 100 per cent is waiting in the wings, he's on his way. It is important not to settle for less. If they follow my advice, they will have a new friend and before long a true love. Don't settle for less.

Accept no substitutes! Everyone wins, if you are true to yourself. Stay open to having it all. It's what you deserve.

Exercise

Today, affirm you can have a 100 per cent relationship. Enjoy your new connections.

Trust yourself and trust the process.

If you stand empty-handed with trust and joy, your beauty only grows. If a Mr or Ms 85 per cent shows up, enjoy the friendship but hold out for having it all. Mr or Ms 100 per cent is close behind.

DAY 30

The path of relationships

The path of relationships is the quickest path of growth, accomplishing what would take hundreds of years of fighting temptations or decades of meditation, in a much shorter time frame.

Everything between you and your wholeness, the realisation of oneness, will come up in your relationship. Every bit of unfinished business with family members, old loves, friends, etc. will come up disguised as problems in the here and now of relationships. If you adopt the right attitude you will soon recognise the process is healing and helping you to mature. And you will swiftly learn your partner is not your enemy.

Give up your need to be special. Stop attacking your partner because of your or his or her needs, or blaming your partner for what *you* are doing.

A relationship teaches you to receive and to be a partner, which is crucial for your mental, emotional and spiritual growth.

As you partner with your mate, you learn to partner with your Higher Mind and to allow the power of grace to come into your life. Rather than having to 'do' everything yourself, 'doing' with the grace of the

Higher Mind means it will be accomplished easily.

The truth is it is easy to find your perfect mate but much harder to keep him or her! Finding your perfect mate is the beginning of a great adventure in love and consciousness.

Exercise

Decide now that you are going to find – and keep – your perfect mate. Focus on becoming an expert on the path of relationships so your love will create miracles. Choose the path of relationships to accelerate your own healing and growth. Intend that your perfect partner comes to you as part of your healing path.

Choose to commit with your partner to realise your wholeness rather than making your relationship the battleground of specialness and needs.

Choose now to develop a relationship with your Higher Mind, for that will naturally lead you into openness, partnership and living a life of grace.

The great adventure has just begun. May you choose to have smooth sailing. And may your story be a happy one!

ACKNOWLEDGEMENTS

Any book is truly a family project. After all, the family gives the writer to the world. I want to express gratitude for the loving support of my wife, Lency, who first edited the book, and our two children, Christopher and J'aime. I want to thank Peggy Chang for typing and general support, Fred Perry for being the original editor, and Sam Westmacott for her refinement of the work. I acknowledge A Course in Miracles for the seminal healing and teaching it has provided in my life, and I would further like to acknowledge my clients, workshop participants and past girlfriends who have given me so much and taught me so much over the years. And lastly, once again, thank Lency, my wife, partner and true mate. Where would I be without you?

PSYCHOLOGY OF VISION

Developed by Chuck Spezzano and Lency Spezzano, the Psychology of Vision is a therapeutic model based on relationships, leadership and spirituality. Its key aspects centre about the evolutionary progress, change and the purpose of the individual and humanity. Psychology of Vision is a path of the heart that transcends cultural and religious differences by focusing on that which is essential to human experience. For information about other publications and world lectures or seminars contact: Paul Woolf, International Business Manager, PO Box 600, Aylesbury, Bucks. HP18 0UL.
Tel: 01296 770122. E-mail: pwoolf@nildram.co.uk

Also by Chuck Spezzano and published by Arthur James:

If It Hurts It Isn't Love

30 Days to Getting Along with Absolutely Anyone

30 Days to Letting Go of Heartbreak and Attachment